CW00497913

COOKING WITH RICE AND GRAINS

RE-IMAGINING BROWN RICE, QUINOA, AND LENTILS

By
Chef Maggie Chow
Copyright © 2015 by Saxonberg Associates
All rights reserved

Published by
BookSumo, a division of Saxonberg Associates
http://www.booksumo.com/

INTRODUCTION

Welcome to *The Effortless Chef Series*! Thank you for taking the time to download the *Easy Rice and Grains Cookbook*. Come take a journey with me into the delights of easy cooking. The point of this cookbook and all my cookbooks is to exemplify the effortless nature of cooking simply.

In this book we focus on cooking with Rice and Grains. You will find that even though the recipes are simple, the taste of the dishes is quite amazing.

So will you join me in an adventure of simple cooking? If the answer is yes (and I hope it is) please consult the table of contents to find the dishes you are most interested in. Once you are ready jump right in and start cooking.

— Chef Maggie Chow

TABLE OF CONTENTS

Any Issues? Contact Me

If you find that something important to you is missing from this book please contact me at maggie@booksumo.com.

I will try my best to re-publish a revised copy taking your feedback into consideration and let you know when the book has been revised with you in mind.

:)

— Chef Maggie Chow

Legal Notes

ALL RIGHTS RESERVED. NO PART OF THIS BOOK MAY BE REPRODUCED OR TRANSMITTED IN ANY FORM OR BY ANY MEANS. PHOTOCOPYING, POSTING ONLINE, AND / OR DIGITAL COPYING IS STRICTLY PROHIBITED UNLESS WRITTEN PERMISSION IS GRANTED BY THE BOOK'S PUBLISHING COMPANY. LIMITED USE OF THE BOOK'S TEXT IS PERMITTED FOR USE IN REVIEWS WRITTEN FOR THE PUBLIC AND/OR PUBLIC DOMAIN.

COMMON ABBREVIATIONS

cup(s)	C.
tablespoon	tbsp
teaspoon	tsp
ounce	oz.
pound	lb

*All units used are standard American measurements

CHAPTER 1: COOKING WITH RICE

RICE DESSERT

Ingredients

- 3/4 C. uncooked white rice
- 2 C. milk, divided
- 1/3 C. white sugar
- 1/4 tsp salt
- 1 egg, beaten
- 2/3 C. golden raisins
- 1 tbsp butter
- 1/2 tsp vanilla extract

Directions

- Get a saucepan add in your rice, and also 1.5 C. of water.
- Bring everything to a rolling boil. Once boiling set the heat to low. Place a lid on the pot and let the rice cook for 22 mins.
- Get a 2nd pot, combine in it: salt, 1.5 C. cooked rice, sugar, and 1.5 C. milk.
- Heat this mix until it gets smooth and cream-like. This should take about 22 mins of cooking and occasional stirring.
- Finally add in: raisins, the rest of your milk, and whisked eggs.
- Heat for another 4 mins. Make sure to keep stirring.
- Add in some vanilla and butter. And let the contents cool before serving.

Amount per serving (4 total)

Timing Information:

Preparation	Cooking	Total Time
25 m	20 m	45 m

Nutritional Information:

Calories	366 kcal
Fat	6.9 g
Carbohydrates	67.6g
Protein	8.8 g
Cholesterol	64 mg
Sodium	237 mg

* Percent Daily Values are based on a 2,000 calorie diet.

South of the Border Style Rice

Ingredients

- 1 lb lean ground beef
- 1 onion, minced
- 1 green bell pepper, minced
- 1 (14 oz.) can beef broth
- 2 C. fresh corn kernels
- 1 (10 oz.) can minced tomatoes with green chili peppers
- 1 (15 oz.) can tomato sauce
- 1/2 C. salsa
- 1/2 tsp chili powder
- 1/2 tsp paprika
- 1/2 tsp garlic powder
- 1/2 tsp salt
- 1/2 tsp ground black pepper
- 1 tsp minced cilantro
- 1 1/2 C. uncooked white rice
- 1 C. shredded Cheddar cheese

Directions

- Fry your beef until fully done. Remove any excess oils or fats. Then mix in your green pepper, and onions. Continue frying until the onions are soft. Add in your tomato sauce, beef broth, chili peppers with tomatoes, and the corn.
- Heat this up for 2 mins. Then mix in: cilantro, salsa, chili powder, pepper, paprika, salt, and garlic powder.
- Combine these contents evenly. Then get everything boiling.
- Once boiling add in your rice.
- Lower the heat.
- Place a lid on the pot and cook the rice for 26 mins until tender.

- After 26 min add some cheddar and cook for another 10 mins.
- Enjoy.

Amount per serving (6 total)

Timing Information:

Preparation	Cooking	Total Time
20 m	35 m	55 m

Nutritional Information:

Calories	510 kcal
Fat	18.3 g
Carbohydrates	59.1g
Protein	28.3 g
Cholesterol	74 mg
Sodium	1294 mg

* Percent Daily Values are based on a 2,000 calorie diet.

PEAS, PIMENTO, AND PICKLED RELISH RICE

Ingredients

- 2 C. water
- 1 C. white rice
- 6 eggs
- 1 (10 oz.) package frozen peas, thawed
- 1 C. diced celery
- 1/4 C. diced onion
- 1 (4 oz.) jar minced pimento
- 1 C. mayonnaise
- 1 tsp prepared mustard
- 1 tbsp lemon juice
- 1/4 C. sweet pickle relish
- 1 (9 oz.) can solid white tuna packed in water, drained
- 1/4 tsp dried dill weed
- 1 tsp salt
- 1/8 tsp pepper

Directions

- Add your rice and some water to a big pot. Get everything to a rolling boil. Once boiling lower the heat. Place a lid on the pot and let the rice cook for 22 mins. Then turn off the heat once the rice is tender.
- Get a 2nd pot. Put your eggs in the pot and add enough cold water to submerge the eggs. Get the water and eggs boiling. Then turn off the heat.
- For 14 mins let the eggs sit in the water to cook. Remove the shells and dice the eggs.
- Clean your peas then get a bowl.

- Put the following in the bowl and evenly mix: pimiento, eggs, onions, rice, and celery.
- Get a 2nd bowl, mix: pepper, mayo, salt, mustard, dill, lemon juice, tuna, and relish.
- Combine both bowls, and evenly mix them. Then chill the mixture in the fridge for 5 hours.
- Enjoy cold.

Amount per serving (8 total)

Timing Information:

Preparation	Cooking	Total Time
20 m	30 m	4 h 50 m

Nutritional Information:

Calories	424 kcal
Fat	26.2 g
Carbohydrates	30.1g
Protein	17.2 g
Cholesterol	159 mg
Sodium	691 mg

* Percent Daily Values are based on a 2,000 calorie diet.

CURRY RICE

Ingredients

- 1 C. jasmine rice
- 2 C. water
- 1 tbsp ghee (clarified butter)
- 1 dried red chili pepper, broken in half (optional)
- 1 tsp black mustard seeds
- 1/2 tsp ground turmeric
- 4 fresh curry leaves
- 1 pinch asafoetida powder (optional)
- 1/4 C. milk
- 1 C. plain yogurt
- salt to taste

Directions

- Get a large pot and add in your rice and cover it with water. Bring the water to a rolling boil. Then set the heat to low. Place a lid on the pot and let the rice cook for 22 mins until soft.
- Get a frying pan and stir fry your chili in ghee for 1 min. Then add in mustard seeds, and cook for another 1 min. Turn off the heat.

- Add in your asafoetida powder, curry leaves, and turmeric spice to your peppers.
- Get a bowl, mix: spicy peppers, yogurt and milk.
- Combine the peppers with the rice and add some salt for seasoning.
- Enjoy at room temp.

Amount per serving (4 total)

Timing Information:

Preparation	Cooking	Total Time
5 m	20 m	1 h 10 m

Nutritional Information:

Calories	271 kcal
Fat	5.2 g
Carbohydrates	48g
Protein	8.1 g
Cholesterol	13 mg
Sodium	76 mg

* Percent Daily Values are based on a 2,000 calorie diet.

NUTTY RICE

Ingredients

- 1 C. brown rice
- 2 tbsps margarine
- 1/4 C. finely diced onion
- 1/2 C. finely diced pecans
- 2 tbsps minced parsley
- 1/4 tsp dried basil
- 1/4 tsp ground ginger
- 1/4 tsp ground black pepper
- 1/4 tsp salt

Directions

- Get a large pot and add your rice to it. Also add about two C. or water. Bring everything to a rolling boil. Then set the heat to low. Place a lid on the pot and cook the rice for 42 mins. Turn off the heat when the rice is tender.
- Simultaneously while the rice is cooking fry the following in margarine: salt, onions, pepper, pecans, ginger, basil, and parsley.
- Stir fry this mix until the onions are soft.
- Add your seasoned onions and pecans to your brown rice and mix evenly.
- Enjoy warm.

Amount per serving (4 total)

Timing Information:

Preparation	Cooking	Total Time
5 m	40 m	45 m

Nutritional Information:

Calories	280 kcal
Fat	16.1 g
Carbohydrates	31g
Protein	4.3 g
Cholesterol	0 mg
Sodium	210 mg

* Percent Daily Values are based on a 2,000 calorie diet.

Long Grain Chicken Flavored Chili Rice

Ingredients

- 1 tbsp vegetable oil
- 1 C. long-grain white rice
- 1 (4 oz.) can diced green chilies
- 1 tsp ground black pepper
- 2 C. chicken broth

Directions

- Get a frying pan hot with veggie oil. Add into the hot oil your chili peppers, and rice.
- Stir fry the rice and peppers for 4 mins to get everything lightly coated and nicely toasted.
- Add in your broth to the peppers, and heat the broth until it is boiling.
- Lower the heat under the pan, place a lid on it, and cook for 22 mins. After the cooking time has elapsed your rice should be tender.
- Enjoy warm.

Amount per serving (6 total)

Timing Information:

Preparation	Cooking	Total Time
10 m	25 m	35 m

Nutritional Information:

Calories	83 kcal
Fat	2.6 g
Carbohydrates	13g
Protein	1.9 g
Cholesterol	2 mg
Sodium	757 mg

* Percent Daily Values are based on a 2,000 calorie diet.

MIDDLE EASTERN STYLE RICE

Ingredients

- 1 1/2 lb lean ground beef
- 3 tbsps garlic powder
- 2 tbsps ground cinnamon
- 1 tbsp ground allspice
- 4 C. water
- 2 C. long-grain rice
- 1 tsp beef bouillon granules
- 1/4 C. pine nuts
- 1 squeeze lemon juice, or to taste

Directions

- Get a frying pan and fry your beef with allspice, garlic powder, and cinnamon, until fully cooked for 12 mins. Crumble the beef after it is done.
- Add the following to your beef, and mix it nicely: beef bouillon, rice, and water. Bring the mixture to a boiling state, then lower the heat and let the rice lightly simmer for 22 mins.
- Simultaneously while the rice is cooking toast your pine nuts with no oil for 5 mins.
- Garnish your rice with some lemon juice and the pine nuts.
- Enjoy immediately.

Amount per serving (6 total)

Timing Information:

Preparation	Cooking	Total Time
5 m	35 m	40 m

Nutritional Information:

Calories	377 kcal
Fat	17.1 g
Carbohydrates	29.5g
Protein	26.6 g
Cholesterol	74 mg
Sodium	584 mg

* Percent Daily Values are based on a 2,000 calorie diet.

RICE CASSEROLE

Ingredients

- 1 lb ground beef
- 1 (26 oz.) jar spaghetti sauce
- 1/2 tsp garlic powder
- 3 C. cooked rice, cooled
- 2 eggs, lightly beaten
- 3/4 C. shredded Parmesan cheese, divided
- 2 1/4 C. shredded mozzarella cheese
- 2 C. cottage cheese

Directions

- Set your oven to 375 degrees before doing anything else.
- Fry your beef for 8 mins and remove any excess oil then crumble it. Add in your garlic powder, and evenly mix everything then add in your tomato sauce, and mix one more time.
- Get a bowl, and combine: eggs, rice, and one fourth a C. of parmesan.
- Get a 2nd bowl, combine: one fourth C. parmesan, cottage cheese, and two C. of mozzarella.
- Get a casserole dish and coat it with nonstick spray, then layer the following: half of your rice, half of your cheese, half of your beef and tomato sauce.

- Continue until the casserole dish is full or all the ingredients are used.
- Cook in the oven for 27 mins. Let the casserole cool.
- Enjoy.

Amount per serving (8 total)

Timing Information:

Preparation	Cooking	Total Time
20 m	25 m	45 m

Nutritional Information:

Calories	461 kcal
Fat	20.3 g
Carbohydrates	35.3g
Protein	32 g
Cholesterol	118 mg
Sodium	975 mg

* Percent Daily Values are based on a 2,000 calorie diet.

WHITE RICE AND TOMATOES

Ingredients

- 1 slice bacon, diced
- 1/2 onion, diced
- 1/4 green bell pepper, diced
- 1/2 tsp diced fresh thyme
- 1/2 C. tomato sauce
- 1 tsp browning sauce
- 1 tsp salt
- 1/2 tsp ground black pepper
- 1 pinch red pepper flakes
- 2 (14 oz.) cans whole kernel corn, drained
- 3 1/2 C. water
- 2 C. white rice

Directions

- Fry your bacon. Then remove any excess oils.
- Combine with the bacon: thyme, onions, and bell peppers.
- Stir fry until the onions are see-through. Lower the heat under the pan and add in: pepper flakes, tomato sauce, black pepper, salt, and browning sauce.

- Cook the sauces for 4 mins. Then combine in your water and stir everything. Increase the heat to get the water and sauces boiling. Once boiling add in your rice, then stir it, then lower the heat again.
- Place a lid on the pan and cook the rice for 32 mins.
- Stir your rice after it is done and enjoy warm.

Amount per serving (5 total)

Timing Information:

Preparation	Cooking	Total Time
20 m	50 m	1 h 10 m

Nutritional Information:

Calories	422 kcal
Fat	2.8 g
Carbohydrates	92g
Protein	10.7 g
Cholesterol	2 mg
Sodium	1120 mg

* Percent Daily Values are based on a 2,000 calorie diet.

Rice from Frankfurt

Ingredients

- 1/4 C. olive oil
- 1 1/2 lb fresh bratwurst links, casings removed
- 1 onion, halved and thinly sliced into half rings
- 1 tsp minced garlic
- 2 tsps fennel seed
- 1 (14.5 oz.) can Bavarian-style sauerkraut, undrained
- 3 C. uncooked white rice
- 1 tbsp chicken soup base (paste)
- 6 C. water
- 1 tsp ground black pepper
- 1/4 C. raisins

Directions

- Stir fry your bratwurst in olive oil until browned. Then crumble it. Fry for about 12 mins.
- Now add in your garlic and onions and continue stir frying for 7 more mins.
- Combine in your sauerkraut and it's juice, and also your fennel seeds. Continue stir frying for 1 more min.
- Add soup base and the rice and evenly mix everything for 2 mins.

- Finally add in your raisins, water, and black pepper.
- Turn up the heat to get everything boiling.
- Boil for 6 mins. Then set the heat to low and cook the rice for 30 mins with a light simmer.
- Enjoy.

Amount per serving (7 total)

Timing Information:

Preparation	Cooking	Total Time
15 m	50 m	1 h 5 m

Nutritional Information:

Calories	716 kcal
Fat	35.2 g
Carbohydrates	79g
Protein	19 g
Cholesterol	59 mg
Sodium	1633 mg

* Percent Daily Values are based on a 2,000 calorie diet.

JALAPENO AND CREAM RICE

Ingredients

- 1/3 C. uncooked long grain white rice
- 2/3 C. water
- 1 (10.75 oz.) can condensed cream of chicken soup, undiluted
- 1/4 C. milk
- 2 fresh jalapeno peppers, seeded and diced
- 1/2 tsp salt
- 1/4 tsp ground black pepper
- 2 tbsps butter
- 1/2 C. diced onion
- 1 (10 oz.) package frozen diced spinach, thawed and drained
- 4 oz. processed cheese food, cubed

Directions

- Get a casserole dish and coat it with nonstick spray or oil and set your oven to 375 degrees before doing anything else.
- Get a saucepan and add in your water and rice. Bring the water to a rolling boil and then set the heat to low and place a lid on the pot. Cook the rice for 22 mins.
- Get a bowl and evenly mix: pepper, soup, salt, jalapenos, and milk.

- Fry your onions in melted butter until soft. Then add in your spinach. Cook for 1 more min. Then combine in your cooked rice.
- Finally add in your soup and heat everything up. Add the cheese and then dump everything into your greased casserole dish.
- Cook the casserole in the oven for 27 mins. Let the contents cool.
- Enjoy.

Amount per serving (6 total)

Timing Information:

Preparation	Cooking	Total Time
15 m	45 m	1 h

Nutritional Information:

Calories	207 kcal
Fat	12.1 g
Carbohydrates	17.9g
Protein	7.8 g
Cholesterol	30 mg
Sodium	830 mg

* Percent Daily Values are based on a 2,000 calorie diet.

EASY ORZO STYLE

Ingredients

- 2 tbsps butter
- 1/2 C. uncooked orzo pasta
- 1/2 C. long-grain white rice
- 1 cube chicken bouillon
- 2 C. water

Directions

- Fry your orzo in melted butter, in a saucepan, until toasted nicely. Then add in your bouillon, water, and rice.
- Get the water boiling then lower the heat. Place a lid on the pan. Cook for 25 to 30 mins.
- Enjoy warm.

Amount per serving (5 total)

Timing Information:

Preparation	Cooking	Total Time
5 m	25 m	30 m

Nutritional Information:

Calories	192 kcal
Fat	5.1 g
Carbohydrates	31.7g
Protein	4.6 g
Cholesterol	12 mg
Sodium	265 mg

* Percent Daily Values are based on a 2,000 calorie diet.

LOUISIANA RICE

Ingredients

- 1 lb lean ground beef
- 1 lb beef sausage
- 1 onion, finely minced
- 1 (8 oz.) package dirty rice mix
- 2 C. water

- 1 (10 oz.) can diced tomatoes with green chili peppers
- 2 (15 oz.) cans kidney beans, drained
- salt and pepper to taste

Directions

- Stir fry your onions, sausage, and beef. Until the meats are fully cooked. Remove any excess oils.
- Get a saucepan and add in your water and rice along with: kidney beans, chilies and tomatoes.
- Heat everything with high heat until boiling, then add in your meats and onions.
- Get everything boiling again. Then combine in some pepper and salt.
- Place a lid on the pan and set the heat to low and cook for 27 mins until the rice is nice and soft.
- Fluff the rice and enjoy.

Amount per serving (8 total)

Timing Information:

Preparation	Cooking	Total Time
15 m	35 m	50 m

Nutritional Information:

Calories	485 kcal
Fat	23.5 g
Carbohydrates	41.4g
Protein	26.2 g
Cholesterol	72 mg
Sodium	1541 mg

* Percent Daily Values are based on a 2,000 calorie diet.

Easy Meaty Rice

Ingredients

- 1 lb ground beef
- 1 (6.9 oz.) package chicken flavored rice mix
- 2 C. water

Directions

- Fry your beef until fully done and then crumble it and remove any excess oils. This should take about 8 mins.
- Add your rice to the beef and toast it for 6 mins.
- Combine in the water and packet seasonings and place a lid on the skillet.
- Get all the contents boiling and then set the heat to low and cook the rice for 30 mins.
- Enjoy.

Amount per serving (4 total)

Timing Information:

Preparation	Cooking	Total Time
5 m	40 m	45 m

Nutritional Information:

Calories	361 kcal
Fat	14 g
Carbohydrates	35.5g
Protein	23.8 g
Cholesterol	69 mg
Sodium	814 mg

* Percent Daily Values are based on a 2,000 calorie diet.

MAGGIE'S FAVORITE RICE

Ingredients

- 1 tbsp butter, or as needed
- 3 C. cooked rice, or more to taste
- 2 C. sour cream
- 1 lb shredded Monterey Jack cheese
- 2 (4 oz.) cans diced green chilies
- 1/2 C. grated Cheddar cheese
- salt to taste

Directions

- Coat a baking dish with butter and set your oven to 350 degrees before doing anything else.
- Add to the baking dish the following (in order): rice, salt, sour cream, green chilies, and Monterey. Top with some cheddar.
- Cook for 32 mins in the oven. Let the contents cool.
- Enjoy.

Amount per serving (8 total)

Timing Information:

Preparation	Cooking	Total Time
10 m	30 m	40 m

Nutritional Information:

Calories	465 kcal
Fat	33.7 g
Carbohydrates	21.1g
Protein	19.7 g
Cholesterol	89 mg
Sodium	747 mg

* Percent Daily Values are based on a 2,000 calorie diet.

BEEF AND ONION RICE

Ingredients

- 1/4 C. butter
- 1 1/4 C. long-grain rice
- 2 (10.5 oz.) cans beef consommé
- 1/2 tsp salt
- 3/4 C. diced green onions
- 3/4 C. diced carrots
- 3/4 C. diced celery
- 1/4 C. sliced almonds

Directions

- Set your oven to 375 degrees before doing anything else.
- For 5 mins fry your rice in melted butter until toasted and browned. Add some salt and your consommé over the rice and get everything boiling. Once boiling enter the contents into a baking dish.
- Cook the rice in the oven for 30 mins. Then add in come almonds, green onions, celery, and carrots to the rice and stir it nicely. Place it back in the oven for 5 more mins.
- Enjoy.

Amount per serving (6 total)

Timing Information:

Preparation	Cooking	Total Time
15 m	40 m	55 m

Nutritional Information:

Calories	269 kcal
Fat	10 g
Carbohydrates	35.9g
Protein	8.5 g
Cholesterol	20 mg
Sodium	792 mg

* Percent Daily Values are based on a 2,000 calorie diet.

Parsley Butter Rice

Ingredients

- 1 tbsp butter
- 1 C. diced onion
- 1 clove garlic, minced
- 1 C. minced green bell pepper
- 3 1/3 C. water
- 1 1/2 C. converted rice
- 1/2 tsp dried parsley
- 1 bay leaf

Directions

- Fry your onions for 5 mins in melted butter until see-through, in a saucepan.
- Add the garlic into the onions and cook for another 3 mins.
- Add in bell peppers and cook for 2 more mins.
- Finally combine with the peppers and onions: water, bay leaf, parsley and rice.
- Bring everything to a rolling boil and once boiling place a lid on the pot, set the heat to low, and then cook the rice for 22 mins until soft.
- Let the contents cool for a bit.
- Enjoy.

Amount per serving (6 total)

Timing Information:

Preparation	Cooking	Total Time
15 m	30 m	50 m

Nutritional Information:

Calories	131 kcal
Fat	2.4 g
Carbohydrates	24.7g
Protein	2.4 g
Cholesterol	5 mg
Sodium	23 mg

* Percent Daily Values are based on a 2,000 calorie diet.

LATIN STYLE RICE

Ingredients

- 3 tbsps butter
- 1 C. diced onions
- 1 C. diced green bell pepper
- 1/2 C. diced celery
- 1 clove garlic, minced
- 1 (28 oz.) can minced tomatoes with juice
- 2 tsps chili powder
- 2 tsps beef bouillon granules
- 1/2 tsp salt
- 3 C. cooked white rice

Directions

- Stir fry the following in butter: garlic, onions, celery, and green bell peppers for 12 mins.
- Add in your rice, salt, tomatoes with juice, beef bouillon, and chili powder.
- Heat until lightly boiling and let the contents simmer for 22 mins until the rice is tender.
- Enjoy.

Amount per serving (6 total)

Timing Information:

Preparation	Cooking	Total Time
15 m	20 m	35 m

Nutritional Information:

Calories	203 kcal
Fat	6.3 g
Carbohydrates	31.4g
Protein	4.1 g
Cholesterol	15 mg
Sodium	607 mg

* Percent Daily Values are based on a 2,000 calorie diet.

Easy Persian Style Rice

Ingredients

- 2 C. uncooked long-grain rice
- 3/4 tsp crushed saffron threads
- 4 tbsps butter
- 6 whole cardamom seeds
- 4 whole cloves
- 3 cinnamon sticks
- 1 onion, chopped
- 3 C. boiling vegetable broth
- 1 tsp salt

Directions

- Soak your rice in a bowl covered in cold water for 32 mins.
- Get a 2nd bowl, and soak your saffron in 2 tbsps of boiling water.
- Stir fry your cinnamon, cardamom, and cloves for 3 mins, then combine in onions and fry until they are browned. Once the onions are browned add in your rice and let it simmer for 7 mins.
- Add in your broth at this point and let it boil.
- Then add in your saffron water and some salt. Place a lid on the pan and set the heat to low and let the rice cook for 40 mins.

Amount per serving (5 total)

Timing Information:

Preparation	Cooking	Total Time
10 m	40 m	1 h 20 m

Nutritional Information:

Calories	404 kcal
Fat	10.2 g
Carbohydrates	69.5g
Protein	7.1 g
Cholesterol	24 mg
Sodium	812 mg

* Percent Daily Values are based on a 2,000 calorie diet.

Bacon, Apples, and Mushroom White Rice

Ingredients

- 3 C. water
- 1 1/2 C. uncooked white rice
- 3 slices bacon
- 1/2 onion, chopped
- 2 stalks celery, diced
- 1 carrot, chopped
- 1/2 C. peas
- 1 C. fresh mushrooms, sliced
- 1/2 C. slivered almonds
- 1/2 C. raisins
- 1 Granny Smith apple - peeled, cored and diced
- 1 C. cooked, chopped turkey meat
- 1 tsp chicken soup base
- 3 tbsps soy sauce
- 1/2 C. chopped parsley
- ground black pepper to taste

Directions

- Get a large pot and get some water boiling in it. Then mix in your rice. Once boiling set the heat to low, place a lid on the pot and let the rice cook for 20 mins.
- Fry your bacon until crispy and remove any excess oils. Then add in your apple, onions, raisins, celery, almonds, mushrooms, peas, and carrots.
- Continually stir over a lower heat until tender.

- Finally add in the following: pepper, rice, turkey, parsley, chicken soup base, and soy sauce. Mix everything evenly.
- Enjoy.

Amount per serving (12 total)

Timing Information:

Preparation	Cooking	Total Time
15 m	30 m	45 m

Nutritional Information:

Calories	209 kcal
Fat	7 g
Carbohydrates	28.6g
Protein	8.4 g
Cholesterol	14 mg
Sodium	388 mg

* Percent Daily Values are based on a 2,000 calorie diet.

Basmati Peas and Peanut Rice

Ingredients

- 1 C. uncooked basmati rice
- 2 1/4 C. water
- 1/2 tsp salt
- 1/4 tsp ground turmeric
- 1/2 C. frozen petite peas, thawed
- 1/2 C. dry roasted peanuts

Directions

- Bring the following to a rolling boil: turmeric, rice, salt, and water. Once boiling set the heat to low, place a lid on the pot, and let the rice cook for 22 mins.
- After the cooking time has elapsed add in your peanuts and then your peas. Mix everything nicely.
- Then serve once the peas have been warmed.

Amount per serving (4 total)

Timing Information:

Preparation	Cooking	Total Time
10 m	20 m	30 m

Nutritional Information:

Calories	302 kcal
Fat	9.5 g
Carbohydrates	45.7g
Protein	9 g
Cholesterol	0 mg
Sodium	318 mg

* Percent Daily Values are based on a 2,000 calorie diet.

LONGHORN BEEF AND CHEDDAR RICE

Ingredients

- 3 C. water
- 2 C. uncooked long grain white rice
- 6 slices bacon
- 1 1/2 lb ground beef
- 1 onion, chopped
- 1/2 green bell pepper, seeded and chopped
- 1 (28 oz.) can peeled and diced tomatoes
- 1 1/2 tsps salt
- 1/4 tsp ground black pepper
- 1 1/2 C. shredded Cheddar cheese

Directions

- Set your oven to 400 degrees before doing anything else.
- Bring the following to a rolling boil: water and rice.
- Set the heat to low and then place a lid on the pot and let the rice cook for 22 mins until tender.
- Fry your bacon simultaneously until crispy.
- Set aside 2 tbsps of oil. Then crumble the bacon.

- Once the bacon is crumbled remove it from the pan and add in: onions, ground beef, and green peppers.
- Cook everything until the beef is fully done.
- Then remove all excess oils and add some pepper and salt for taste.
- Now grab a casserole dish and put the rice and beef mix into it.
- Then add bacon, beef mix, bacon oil, and tomatoes.
- Combine everything nicely.
- Then garnish the dish with some cheddar.
- Cook in the oven for 35 mins.
- Enjoy.

Amount per serving (10 total)

Timing Information:

Preparation	Cooking	Total Time
30 m	30 m	1 h

Nutritional Information:

Calories	391 kcal
Fat	17.4 g
Carbohydrates	33.9g
Protein	22 g
Cholesterol	69 mg
Sodium	771 mg

* Percent Daily Values are based on a 2,000 calorie diet.

WEST AFRICAN STYLE RICE

Ingredients

- 1 tbsp olive oil
- 1 large onion, sliced
- 2 (14.5 oz.) cans stewed tomatoes
- 1/2 (6 oz.) can tomato paste
- 1 tsp salt
- 1/4 tsp black pepper
- 1/4 tsp cayenne pepper
- 1/2 tsp red pepper flakes
- 1 tbsp Worcestershire sauce

- 1 tsp chopped fresh rosemary
- 2 C. water
- 1 (3 lbs) whole chicken, cut into 8 pieces
- 1 C. uncooked white rice
- 1 C. diced carrots
- 1/2 pound fresh green beans, trimmed and snapped into 1 to 2 inch pieces
- 1/4 tsp ground nutmeg

Directions

- Fry your onions in oil until they are see-through. Then add in tomato paste and tomato sauce, rosemary, salt, cayenne, red pepper flakes, and Worchestshire.
- Bring everything to a rolling boil, then set the heat low, put in the water and the chicken pieces, and place a lid on the pot. Let the chicken simmer for 35 mins.
- After 35 mins of simmering add in green beans, nutmeg, rice and carrots.
- Get everything boiling again with high heat and then lower the heat.

- Place a lid back on the pot and let the rice cook for 27 mins until soft.
- Enjoy.

Amount per serving (8 total)

Timing Information:

Preparation	Cooking	Total Time
20 m	1 h	1 h 20 m

Nutritional Information:

Calories	332 kcal
Fat	13.4 g
Carbohydrates	33.5g
Protein	19.8 g
Cholesterol	46 mg
Sodium	713 mg

* Percent Daily Values are based on a 2,000 calorie diet.

CHILI AND CILANTRO JASMINE

Ingredients

- 4 tbsps vegetable oil
- 5 cloves garlic, finely chopped
- 2 green chilies, diced
- 2 C. cubed skinless, boneless chicken breast meat
- 2 C. cooked jasmine rice, chilled
- 1 tbsp white sugar
- 1 tbsp fish sauce
- 1 tbsp soy sauce
- 2 tsps chopped green onion
- 2 tbsps chopped fresh basil leaves
- 5 tbsps chopped fresh cilantro

Directions

- Fry your garlic in a wok in oil and then add your chicken, and chili peppers. Stir fry until the chicken is fully cooked.
- Once the chicken is cooked add in: soy sauce, sugar, rice, and fish sauce. Stir fry for 2 mins then add in your cilantro, green onions, and basil cook for another 2 mins. Then enjoy.

Amount per serving (4 total)

Timing Information:

Preparation	Cooking	Total Time
15 m	15 m	30 m

Nutritional Information:

Calories	634 kcal
Fat	17.3 g
Carbohydrates	84.4g
Protein	32.8 g
Cholesterol	68 mg
Sodium	562 mg

* Percent Daily Values are based on a 2,000 calorie diet.

Chapter 2: Cooking with Quinoa

Gouda, Spinach, and Sunflowers Quinoa

Ingredients

- 1/4 C. quinoa
- 3 tbsps olive oil
- 2 tbsps raw sunflower seeds
- 2 cloves garlic, minced
- 1/2 C. fresh spinach leaves
- 2 tsps lemon juice
- 1/3 C. grated goat gouda cheese

Directions

- Boil your quinoa in salt and water for 17 mins. Then with a strainer remove all the liquid and clean the quinoa under cold water.
- Toast your sunflower seeds in olive oil for 3 mins then add the garlic and cook for 3 more mins.
- Pour in your quinoa and also the spinach. Stir and heat everything until the spinach is soft.
- Now add your lemon juice and some cheese.
- Continue stirring for a few more mins until the cheese is melted.
- When serving this dish top with more cheese.
- Enjoy.

Amount per serving (3 total)

Timing Information:

Preparation	Cooking	Total Time
10 m	30 m	40 m

Nutritional Information:

Calories	233 kcal
Fat	18.9 g
Carbohydrates	10.5g
Protein	6.1 g
Cholesterol	13 mg
Sodium	49 mg

* Percent Daily Values are based on a 2,000 calorie diet.

CHILI AND CURRY QUINOA

Ingredients

- 2 tbsps olive oil, or as needed
- 1 small onion, diced
- 2 cloves garlic, minced
- 1 C. quinoa
- 2 C. chicken broth
- 1 tbsp curry powder, or to taste
- 1 tbsp ancho chili powder
- salt and pepper to taste

Directions

- Stir fry your garlic and onions in oil for 4 mins then add your quinoa and cook for 6 mins.
- Add in the broth and get everything boiling. Once the quinoa is boiling, add your chili and curry powder, place a lid on the pot, and lower the heat. Let the contents cook for 27 mins.
- Before serving add your preferred amount of pepper and salt.
- Enjoy.

Amount per serving (2 total)

Timing Information:

Preparation	Cooking	Total Time
5 m	35 m	40 m

Nutritional Information:

Calories	473 kcal
Fat	19.8 g
Carbohydrates	62.8g
Protein	13.5 g
Cholesterol	0 mg
Sodium	48 mg

* Percent Daily Values are based on a 2,000 calorie diet.

Maple Syrup, Lemons, and Blueberries Quinoa

(Breakfast Quinoa)

Ingredients

- 1 C. quinoa
- 2 C. nonfat milk
- 1 pinch salt
- 3 tbsps maple syrup
- 1/2 lemon, zested
- 1 C. blueberries
- 1 tsps flax seed

Directions

- Rinse your quinoa under cold water with a strainer until the water runs clear.
- Pour your milk into a big pot and warm it for 3 mins.
- Once the milk is warm add your salt and quinoa.
- Let the contents lightly boil for 22 mins. Then shut the heat and add: lemon zest, syrup, and blueberries.
- Mix everything together to evenly distribute the fruit and syrup.
- When serving your quinoa add a garnishing of flax seeds.
- Enjoy.

Amount per serving (2 total)

Timing Information:

Preparation	Cooking	Total Time
5 m	25 m	30 m

Nutritional Information:

Calories	538 kcal
Fat	7.3 g
Carbohydrates	98.7g
Protein	21.5 g
Cholesterol	5 mg
Sodium	112 mg

* Percent Daily Values are based on a 2,000 calorie diet.

CUCUMBERS, TOMATOES, PARSLEY, AND ONIONS QUINOA

(TABBOULEH)

Ingredients

- 2 C. water
- 1 C. quinoa
- 1 pinch salt
- 1/4 C. olive oil
- 1/2 tsp sea salt
- 1/4 C. lemon juice

- 3 tomatoes, diced
- 1 cucumber, diced
- 2 bunches green onions, diced
- 2 carrots, grated
- 1 C. fresh parsley, chopped

Directions

- Add some salt and quinoa to boiling water.
- Now get the water boiling again with the quinoa in it and place a lid on the pot.
- Set the heat to low and let the contents gently boil for 17 mins.
- Now shut the heat and let the quinoa cool down. Once it has cooled stir it with a large fork.
- Get a bowl, combine: parsley, olive oil, carrots, sea salt, onions, lemon juice, cucumbers, and tomatoes.

- Combine the veggie mix with the quinoa and toss.
- Enjoy.

Amount per serving (4 total)

Timing Information:

Preparation	Cooking	Total Time
15 m	15 m	30 m

Nutritional Information:

Calories	354 kcal
Fat	16.6 g
Carbohydrates	45.7g
Protein	9.6 g
Cholesterol	0 mg
Sodium	383 mg

* Percent Daily Values are based on a 2,000 calorie diet.

BROCCOLI AND CHEDDAR QUINOA

Ingredients

- 2 C. chopped broccoli
- 1 3/4 C. vegetable broth
- 1 C. quinoa
- 1 C. shredded Cheddar cheese
- salt and ground black pepper to taste

Directions

- Boil, in a big pot: quinoa, broccoli, and broth.
- Once boiling place a lid on the pot and lower the heat.
- Let the quinoa gently boil for 17 mins. Then add your cheese.
- Cook everything for 4 more mins until the cheese is melted and then add your preferred amount of pepper and salt.
- Enjoy.

Amount per serving (4 total)

Timing Information:

Preparation	Cooking	Total Time
5 m	20 m	25 m

Nutritional Information:

Calories	299 kcal
Fat	12.3 g
Carbohydrates	32.9g
Protein	14.8 g
Cholesterol	30 mg
Sodium	491 mg

* Percent Daily Values are based on a 2,000 calorie diet.

ALMONDS, RAISINS, CARROTS, AND CELERY QUINOA

Ingredients

- 1/2 C. quinoa, rinsed and drained
- 1 C. cold water
- 1/4 tsp salt
- 3 tbsps olive oil
- 1 celery rib, chopped
- 1 small onion, chopped
- 1 carrot, chopped
- 1 clove garlic, minced
- 8 almonds, coarsely chopped
- 1 small tomato, seeded and chopped
- 2 tbsps raisins
- 1/8 tsp salt
- 1/8 tsp ground black pepper
- 1/8 tsp dried thyme
- 1/8 tsp dried oregano
- 1 pinch coarse sea salt

Directions

- Boil: salt, water, and quinoa.
- Once boiling place a lid on the pot, lower the heat, and let the contents lightly boil for 17 mins.
- Simultaneously stir fry the following, in olive oil, for 8 mins: garlic, celery, carrots, and onions.
- Now add in: thyme, almond, oregano, tomatoes, pepper, salt, and raisins.
- Cook the seasoned mix for 2 more mins.

- Once the quinoa is finished stir it with a fork and then pour the quinoa into the carrot mix.
- For 1 min stir fry the new mix to get the veggies evenly distributed throughout the quinoa.
- When serving the quinoa top with some more sea salt.
- Enjoy.

Amount per serving (3 total)

Timing Information:

Preparation	Cooking	Total Time
20 m	25 m	45 m

Nutritional Information:

Calories	303 kcal
Fat	17.1 g
Carbohydrates	33g
Protein	6.2 g
Cholesterol	0 mg
Sodium	506 mg

* Percent Daily Values are based on a 2,000 calorie diet.

Mangoes and Curry Quinoa

Ingredients

- 1 1/2 C. chicken stock
- 3/4 C. quinoa
- 1 1/2 tsps curry powder
- 1/4 tsp garlic powder
- 1/2 tsp salt
- 1/4 tsp black pepper
- 1 mango - peeled, seeded and diced
- 3 green onions, chopped

Directions

- Boil, in a big pot: pepper, stock, salt, quinoa, garlic powder, and curry powder.
- Once boiling place a lid on the pot, set the heat to low, and let the contents gently cook for 17 mins.
- Let the quinoa loose its heat and add your onions and mangos.
- Now stir everything to evenly distribute the fruit.
- Enjoy.

Amount per serving (4 total)

Timing Information:

Preparation	Cooking	Total Time
10 m	15 m	1 h 25 m

Nutritional Information:

Calories	162 kcal
Fat	2.4 g
Carbohydrates	31.1g
Protein	5.3 g
Cholesterol	1 mg
Sodium	553 mg

* Percent Daily Values are based on a 2,000 calorie diet.

Feta, Zucchini, Basil, and Tomatoes Quinoa

Ingredients

- 1 C. rinsed quinoa
- 2 C. chicken broth
- 2 tbsps extra-virgin olive oil
- 2 garlic scapes, chopped
- 1 small onion, chopped
- 2 skinless, boneless chicken breast halves - cut into strips
- 2 tbsps extra-virgin olive oil
- 1 zucchini, diced
- 1 tomato, diced
- 4 oz. crumbled feta cheese
- 8 fresh basil leaves
- 1 tbsp lime juice

Directions

- Boil your quinoa in broth and once it's boiling place a lid on the pot and let the contents gently cook for 14 mins.
- Simultaneously stir fry your onions and garlic for 7 mins, then add the chicken, and cook for 7 more mins.

- Place the contents in a bowl, add in more olive oil (2 tbsps), and stir fry your tomatoes and zucchini for 10 mins.
- Now add the chicken back in to the mix and top everything with: lime juice, basil, and feta.
- Stir fry this mix until the chicken is fully done for about 8 to 12 more mins.
- When serving your quinoa top it with some of the chicken.
- Enjoy.

Amount per serving (4 total)

Timing Information:

Preparation	Cooking	Total Time
30 m	25 m	55 m

Nutritional Information:

Calories	453 kcal
Fat	23.8 g
Carbohydrates	35.3g
Protein	23.8 g
Cholesterol	61 mg
Sodium	841 mg

* Percent Daily Values are based on a 2,000 calorie diet.

PEPPER, TOMATOES, AND CHILI QUINOA

Ingredients

- 2 tbsps vegetable oil
- 1 C. uncooked quinoa
- 1 medium onion, finely chopped
- 3 cloves garlic, minced
- 1 small green bell pepper, chopped
- 1 (8 oz.) can tomato sauce
- 2 1/2 C. water
- 1 tsp chili powder
- 1/4 tsp garlic powder
- 1/4 tsp ground cumin

Directions

- Stir fry, in veggie oil, for 9 mins: green peppers, quinoa, garlic, and onions.
- Now add: cumin, garlic powder, and chili power.
- Stir the spices in and then add: tomato sauce and water.
- Get everything boiling and then place a lid on the pot and let the contents gently cook with a lower level of heat for 32 mins.
- Every 5 to 10 mins stir your quinoa.
- Enjoy.

Amount per serving (8 total)

Timing Information:

Preparation	Cooking	Total Time
20 m	40 m	1 h

Nutritional Information:

Calories	126 kcal
Fat	4.9 g
Carbohydrates	17.5g
Protein	3.7 g
Cholesterol	0 mg
Sodium	154 mg

* Percent Daily Values are based on a 2,000 calorie diet.

BLACK BEANS AND CORN QUINOA

Ingredients

- 1 tsp vegetable oil
- 1 onion, chopped
- 3 cloves garlic, chopped
- 3/4 C. quinoa
- 1 1/2 C. vegetable broth
- 1 tsp ground cumin
- 1/4 tsp cayenne pepper
- salt and ground black pepper to taste
- 1 C. frozen corn kernels
- 2 (15 oz.) cans black beans, rinsed and drained
- 1/2 C. chopped fresh cilantro

Directions

- Stir fry your garlic and onions in oil for 12 mins then pour in your quinoa and the broth. Stir the contents and then add: pepper, cumin, salt, and cayenne.
- Get everything boiling and once boiling place a lid on the pot, and let the contents gently cook over low heat for 22 mins.

- Now add your corn and keep heating for 7 more mins finally add the cilantro and beans. Cook for a few more mins to heat up the beans. Stir everything before serving.
- Enjoy.

Amount per serving (10 total)

Timing Information:

Preparation	Cooking	Total Time
15 m	35 m	50 m

Nutritional Information:

Calories	153 kcal
Fat	1.7 g
Carbohydrates	27.8g
Protein	7.7 g
Cholesterol	0 mg
Sodium	517 mg

* Percent Daily Values are based on a 2,000 calorie diet.

Turkey Loaf Quinoa

Ingredients

- 1/4 C. quinoa
- 1/2 C. water
- 1 tsp olive oil
- 1 small onion, chopped
- 1 large clove garlic, chopped
- 1 (20 oz.) package ground turkey
- 1 tbsp tomato paste
- 1 tbsp hot pepper sauce
- 2 tbsps Worcestershire sauce
- 1 egg
- 1 1/2 tsps salt
- 1 tsp ground black pepper
- 2 tbsps brown sugar
- 2 tsps Worcestershire sauce
- 1 tsp water

Directions

- Get your quinoa boiling in water and then place a lid on the pot, lower the heat, and let the contents gently boil with a low heat for 17 mins.
- Place everything the side.
- Now set your oven to 350 degrees before doing anything else.
- Stir fry your onions in olive oil for 7 mins then combine in the garlic and cook for 2 more mins.
- Now place this to the side as well.
- Get a bowl, combine: pepper, turkey, salt, quinoa, egg, onions, Worcestershire (2 tbsps), tomato paste, and hot sauce.

- Get a 2nd bowl, mix: remaining Worcestershire, brown sugar, and 1 tsp of water.
- Form the mixture in the 1st bowl into a loaf and place it in a casserole dish coated with nonstick spray. Then top the loaf with the contents of the 2nd bowl.
- Cook the loaf in the oven for 52 mins.
- Check the internal temperature. It should read 160 degrees.
- Cut up your loaf after letting it sit for 13 mins.
- Enjoy.

Amount per serving (5 total)

Timing Information:

Preparation	Cooking	Total Time
30 m	50 m	1 h 20 m

Nutritional Information:

Calories	259 kcal
Fat	11 g
Carbohydrates	15.2g
Protein	25.3 g
Cholesterol	121 mg
Sodium	968 mg

* Percent Daily Values are based on a 2,000 calorie diet.

PINE NUTS AND LEMONS QUINOA

Ingredients

- 1/4 C. pine nuts
- 1 C. quinoa
- 2 C. water
- sea salt to taste
- 1/4 C. fresh lemon juice
- 2 stalks celery, chopped
- 1/4 red onion, chopped
- 1/4 tsp cayenne pepper
- 1/2 tsp ground cumin
- 1 bunch fresh parsley, chopped

Directions

- Toast your pine nuts for 6 mins, make sure you stir vigorously. Then place them to the side.
- Boil your quinoa in water and salt for 12 mins uncovered. At this point the water should have been absorbed if not cook the quinoa for more time.
- Place the quinoa in a bowl and add: parsley, pine nuts, cumin, lemon juice, cayenne, celery, and onions.
- Enjoy with some pepper and salt.

Amount per serving (6 total)

Timing Information:

Preparation	Cooking	Total Time
15 m	10 m	25 m

Nutritional Information:

Calories	147 kcal
Fat	4.8 g
Carbohydrates	21.4g
Protein	5.9 g
Cholesterol	0 mg
Sodium	74 mg

* Percent Daily Values are based on a 2,000 calorie diet.

Quinoa Chili II

Ingredients

- 1 C. uncooked quinoa, rinsed
- 2 C. water
- 1 lb extra lean ground beef
- 1 tbsp olive oil
- 1 onion, chopped
- 4 cloves garlic, minced
- 1 jalapeno pepper, seeded and minced
- 1 tbsp chili powder
- 1 tbsp ground cumin
- 1 (28 oz.) can crushed tomatoes
- 2 (19 oz.) cans black beans, rinsed and drained
- 1 green bell pepper, chopped
- 1 red bell pepper, chopped
- 1 zucchini, chopped (optional)
- 1 tsp dried oregano leaves
- 1 tsp dried parsley
- salt and ground black pepper to taste
- 1 C. frozen corn kernels, thawed
- 1/4 C. chopped fresh cilantro

Directions

- Boil your quinoa in water. Place a lid on the pot, lower the heat, and let it gently boil for 17 mins.
- Stir fry your beef and then remove any excess oils before adding in: jalapenos, garlic, and onions and cooking for 7 more mins.
- Add the chili powder and cumin and cook for 2 more mins.
- Now add: parsley, salt, tomatoes, black pepper, oregano, beans, zucchini, and bell peppers.

- Cook for 22 mins until the peppers are soft.
- Now add the quinoa, corn, and beef.
- Cook for 7 more mins before adding in the cilantro.
- Enjoy.

Amount per serving (8 total)

Timing Information:

Preparation	Cooking	Total Time
30 m	35 m	1 h 5 m

Nutritional Information:

Calories	412 kcal
Fat	11.5 g
Carbohydrates	52.8g
Protein	27.5 g
Cholesterol	45 mg
Sodium	705 mg

* Percent Daily Values are based on a 2,000 calorie diet.

Chapter 3: Cooking with Lentils

Lentil Curry

Ingredients

- 2 C. red lentils
- 1 large onion, diced
- 1 tbsp vegetable oil
- 2 tbsps curry paste
- 1 tbsp curry powder
- 1 tsp ground turmeric
- 1 tsp ground cumin
- 1 tsp chili powder
- 1 tsp salt
- 1 tsp white sugar
- 1 tsp minced garlic
- 1 tsp minced fresh ginger
- 1 (14.25 oz.) can tomato puree

Directions

- Rinse your lentils and then put them in a saucepan submerged in fresh water.
- Get everything boiling and place a lid on the pot and cook it with a low level of heat for 22 mins.
- Now remove all the liquid.
- Get a bowl, combine until smooth: ginger, curry paste, garlic, curry powder, sugar, turmeric, salt, chili powder, and cumin.
- Stir fry your onions in veggie oil for 20 mins and pour in your spice mix.

- Continue stir frying for 2 more mins with a high heat level then add tomato puree and shut the heat.
- Combine the spicy onions with the lentils and stir everything until evenly coated.
- Enjoy.

Amount per serving (8 total)

Timing Information:

Preparation	Cooking	Total Time
10 m	30 m	40 m

Nutritional Information:

Calories	192 kcal
Fat	2.6 g
Carbohydrates	32.5g
Protein	12.1 g
Cholesterol	0 mg
Sodium	572 mg

* Percent Daily Values are based on a 2,000 calorie diet.

Lentils from the Caribbean

Ingredients

- 1/4 C. canola oil
- 1 large onion, diced
- 2 carrots, peeled and diced
- salt and ground black pepper to taste
- 1/2 tsp white sugar
- 3 cloves garlic, minced
- 1 fresh chili pepper, minced
- 1 tsp grated fresh ginger
- 3 tbsps curry powder
- 2 (14 oz.) cans vegetable broth, divided
- 1 C. lentils
- 1/4 C. chopped fresh cilantro, or more to taste

Directions

- Cook your onions for 16 mins in a big pot in canola with the following: sugar, carrots, pepper, and salt. Then set the heat to low and combine in: curry, garlic, ginger, and chili peppers. Stir for 7 mins while heating.
- Turn up the heat on the stove and add 1 can of veggie broth and scrape the pot with a spoon.
- Pour in your lentils and the rest of the broth.
- Cook for 30 mins then add your cilantro.
- Enjoy.

Amount per serving (4 total)

Timing Information:

Preparation	Cooking	Total Time
25 m	50 m	1 h 15 m

Nutritional Information:

Calories	192 kcal
Fat	2.6 g
Carbohydrates	32.5g
Protein	12.1 g
Cholesterol	0 mg
Sodium	572 mg

* Percent Daily Values are based on a 2,000 calorie diet.

LENTIL SOUP I

(RED LENTILS, GARLIC, AND APRICOTS)

Ingredients

- 3 tbsps olive oil
- 1 onion, chopped
- 2 cloves garlic, minced
- 1/3 C. dried apricots
- 1 1/2 C. red lentils
- 5 C. chicken stock

- 3 roma (plum) tomatoes - peeled, seeded and chopped
- 1/2 tsp ground cumin
- 1/2 tsp dried thyme
- salt to taste
- ground black pepper to taste
- 2 tbsps fresh lemon juice

Directions

- In olive oil stir fry your apricots, garlic, and onions for 2 mins. Then add in your stock and lentils and get everything boiling.
- Once boiling, lower the heat and let the contents cook for 30 mins.
- Add in the following after 30 mins: pepper, tomatoes, salt, cumin, and thyme.
- Cook for 12 more mins. Then combine in your lemon juice.
- Ladle out half of the soup and puree it in a blender then pour it back into the main mix.
- Enjoy warm.

Amount per serving (6 total)

Timing Information:

Preparation	Cooking	Total Time
15 m	50 m	1 h 5 m

Nutritional Information:

Calories	263 kcal
Fat	7.4 g
Carbohydrates	37.2g
Protein	13.2 g
Cholesterol	0 mg
Sodium	7 mg

* Percent Daily Values are based on a 2,000 calorie diet.

Lentil Soup II (Onions, Parmesan, and Wine)

(Hungarian Style Lentils)

Ingredients

- 2 tbsps olive oil
- 2 large onions, cubed
- 1 tsp minced garlic
- 3 carrots, diced
- 2 stalks celery, diced
- 3 1/2 C. crushed tomatoes
- 1 1/2 C. lentils - soaked, rinsed and drained
- 1/2 tsp salt
- 1/2 tsp ground black pepper
- 3/4 C. white wine
- 2 bay leaves
- 7 C. chicken stock
- 1 sprig fresh parsley, chopped
- 1/2 tsp paprika
- 1/2 C. grated Parmesan cheese

Directions

- Stir fry your onions in a big pot until translucent then add in: carrots, garlic, celery, and paprika. Continue stir frying for 12 mins.
- Add in: pepper, tomatoes, salt, stock, bay leaves, and lentils. Mix the lentils a bit then pour in your wine and get the mixture boiling. Once everything is

boiling set the heat to low and let the mix simmer for 1 hr. Then add parmesan and parsley.

- Enjoy.

Amount per serving (8 total)

Timing Information:

Preparation	Cooking	Total Time
10 m	1 h 30 m	1 h 40 m

Nutritional Information:

Calories	255 kcal
Fat	6 g
Carbohydrates	33.3g
Protein	13.7 g
Cholesterol	9 mg
Sodium	1099 mg

* Percent Daily Values are based on a 2,000 calorie diet.

Mexican Style Lentils

Ingredients

- 1 tsp canola oil
- 2/3 C. finely chopped onion
- 1 small clove garlic, minced
- 2/3 C. dried lentils, rinsed
- 1 tbsp taco seasoning, or to taste
- 1 2/3 C. chicken broth
- 2/3 C. salsa
- 12 taco shells

Directions

- For 7 mins stir fry your onions in oil then add in your taco seasoning and stir everything before adding the lentils and cooking for 1 more min.
- Add your broth and get everything boiling.
- Once boiling, set the heat to low, and cook for 30 mins with a lid on the pot.
- Remove the lid and cook for 7 more mins to get it thicker then shut the heat and mash everything.
- Now add in the salsa and mix everything nicely.
- Divide the mix amongst your tacos and serve.
- Enjoy.

Amount per serving (6 total)

Timing Information:

Preparation	Cooking	Total Time
10 m	40 m	50 m

Nutritional Information:

Calories	304 kcal
Fat	10 g
Carbohydrates	44.2g
Protein	9.4 g
Cholesterol	1 mg
Sodium	714 mg

* Percent Daily Values are based on a 2,000 calorie diet.

Lentil Soup III (Red Lentils, Sweet Potatoes, and Ginger)

Ingredients

- 1/4 C. butter
- 2 large sweet potatoes, peeled and chopped
- 3 large carrots, peeled and chopped
- 1 apple, peeled, cored and chopped
- 1 onion, chopped
- 1/2 C. red lentils
- 1/2 tsp minced fresh ginger
- 1/2 tsp ground black pepper
- 1 tsp salt
- 1/2 tsp ground cumin
- 1/2 tsp chili powder
- 1/2 tsp paprika
- 4 C. vegetable broth
- plain yogurt

Directions

- Stir fry the following in butter in a saucepan: onions, chunked sweet potatoes, apple, and carrots.
- Cook for 12 mins.
- Now add your veggie broth and the following: paprika, lentils, chili powder, ginger, cumin, black pepper, and salt.
- Get everything boiling, place a lid on the pot, and cook for 30 mins with a low heat.

- Puree the soup in batches and then add it to a separate pot or use an immersion blender to puree everything with one pot.
- Get the pureed soup boiling again and then lower the heat and cook for 12 more mins.
- Add a bit more water if the soup is too thick for your liking.
- When serving add a dollop of yogurt.
- Enjoy.

Amount per serving (6 total)

Timing Information:

Preparation	Cooking	Total Time
20 m	50 m	1 h 10 m

Nutritional Information:

Calories	322 kcal
Fat	9 g
Carbohydrates	52.9g
Protein	9 g
Cholesterol	22 mg
Sodium	876 mg

* Percent Daily Values are based on a 2,000 calorie diet.

LENTILS FROM ARABIA

Ingredients

- 1 C. dry lentils, rinsed
- 2 C. water
- 1 tsp salt
- 1 tbsp ground cumin
- 1 tbsp garlic powder
- 3/4 C. white rice, rinsed
- 3/4 C. water
- 1 tsp salt
- 2 tbsps olive oil
- 1/4 C. vegetable oil
- 3 white onions, sliced into 1/4-inch rings

Directions

- Boil, then simmer the following, with a low heat, for 25 mins, in a big pot: garlic powder, 2 C. of water, cumin, and salt (1 tsp).
- Now add in: olive oil, rice, salt (1 tsp), and 3/4 C. of water.
- Put a lid on the pot and cook for 40 mins with a low heat until the rice is soft.
- Simultaneously stir fry your onions in oil for 12 mins then top the lentils with the onions when everything is finished cooking.
- Enjoy.

Amount per serving (6 total)

Timing Information:

Preparation	Cooking	Total Time
15 m	1 h 10 m	1 h 25 m

Nutritional Information:

Calories	371 kcal
Fat	14.4 g
Carbohydrates	49.8g
Protein	11.6 g
Cholesterol	0 mg
Sodium	788 mg

* Percent Daily Values are based on a 2,000 calorie diet.

Lentils from the Mediterranean

Ingredients

- 1 tbsp olive oil
- 1 1/2 lbs lamb shoulder arm chops, cubed, round bones reserved
- 1 tsp salt
- 1/2 tsp ground black pepper
- 1 onion, chopped
- 4 cloves garlic, minced
- 1 C. lentils, picked over and rinsed
- 2 C. chicken broth, or more as needed
- 1 (14 oz.) can diced tomatoes
- 3 carrots, peeled and sliced
- 1/2 tsp dried thyme
- 1/2 tsp dried sage
- 1/2 tsp dried basil
- 2 C. coarsely chopped fresh spinach
- 1 lemon, juiced and zested
- 1/2 C. ricotta cheese, crumbled

Directions

- Stir fry your lamb for 3 mins until browned, in hot oil, then add pepper and salt.
- Cook this mix for 1 more min.
- Now combine in: garlic and onions.
- Cook for 2 more mins while stirring.

- Add the following: basil, lentils, sage, 2 C. broth, thyme, tomatoes, and carrots.
- Get everything boiling and then place a lid on the pot and let the contents lightly boil for 25 mins.
- Add a C. more of broth if necessary then take out the bones from the lamb and add in the spinach and cook for 7 more mins before adding the lemon juice and zest.
- When serving top with cheese.
- Enjoy.

Amount per serving (4 total)

Timing Information:

Preparation	Cooking	Total Time
15 m	40 m	55 m

Nutritional Information:

Calories	572 kcal
Fat	26.7 g
Carbohydrates	46.4g
Protein	39.3 g
Cholesterol	103 mg
Sodium	1049 mg

* Percent Daily Values are based on a 2,000 calorie diet.

Lentil Soup IV (Red Lentils, Coconut, and Tomatoes)

(Vegan Approved)

Ingredients

- 1 tbsp peanut oil
- 1 small onion, chopped
- 1 tbsp minced fresh ginger root
- 1 clove garlic, chopped
- 1 pinch fenugreek seeds
- 1 C. dry red lentils
- 1 C. butternut squash - peeled, seeded, and cubed
- 1/3 C. finely chopped fresh cilantro
- 2 C. water
- 1/2 (14 oz.) can coconut milk
- 2 tbsps tomato paste
- 1 tsp curry powder
- 1 pinch cayenne pepper
- 1 pinch ground nutmeg
- salt and pepper to taste

Directions

- Stir fry, until soft: fenugreek, onions, garlic, and ginger. Then add in: tomato paste, pepper, curry powder, cilantro, salt, water, lentils, cayenne, coconut milk, nutmeg, and squash.
- Get everything boiling and cook for 32 mins. Enjoy.

Amount per serving (4 total)

Timing Information:

Preparation	Cooking	Total Time
15 m	40 m	55 m

Nutritional Information:

Calories	303 kcal
Fat	14.6 g
Carbohydrates	34.2g
Protein	13 g
Cholesterol	0 mg
Sodium	81 mg

* Percent Daily Values are based on a 2,000 calorie diet.

HEARTY HAM AND LENTILS

Ingredients

- 1 C. dried lentils
- 1 C. chopped celery
- 1 C. chopped carrots
- 1 C. chopped onion
- 2 cloves garlic, minced
- 1 1/2 C. diced cooked ham
- 1/2 tsp dried basil
- 1/4 tsp dried thyme
- 1/2 tsp dried oregano
- 1 bay leaf
- 1/4 tsp black pepper
- 32 oz. chicken broth
- 1 C. water
- 8 tsps tomato sauce

Directions

- Add the following to your crock pot: pepper, lentils, bay leaf, celery, oregano, carrots, thyme, onions, basil, ham, and garlic. Pour in the broth and place a lid on the slow cooker. Let the contents cook on low for 12 hours.
- Enjoy.

Amount per serving (6 total)

Timing Information:

Preparation	Cooking	Total Time
20 m	12 h	12 h 20 m

Nutritional Information:

Calories	222 kcal
Fat	6.1 g
Carbohydrates	26.3g
Protein	15.1 g
Cholesterol	20 mg
Sodium	1170 mg

* Percent Daily Values are based on a 2,000 calorie diet.

LENTILS FROM MOROCCO

Ingredients

- 2 onions, chopped
- 2 cloves garlic, minced
- 1 tsp grated fresh ginger
- 6 C. water
- 1 C. red lentils
- 1 (15 oz.) can garbanzo beans, drained
- 1 (19 oz.) can cannellini beans

- 1 (14.5 oz.) can diced tomatoes
- 1/2 C. diced carrots
- 1/2 C. chopped celery
- 1 tsp garam masala
- 1 1/2 tsps ground cardamom
- 1/2 tsp ground cayenne pepper
- 1/2 tsp ground cumin
- 1 tbsp olive oil

Directions

- Stir fry the following, in a saucepan, in olive oil, for 7 mins: ginger, garlic, and onions.
- Pour in your water, cumin, lentils, cayenne, chick peas, cardamom, kidney beans, masala, tomatoes, celery, and carrots.
- Get the mix boiling, then lower the heat for a gentle simmer for 2 hrs.
- Puree about one half of the soup in a blender and then mix it back into the saucepan before serving.
- Enjoy.

Amount per serving (6 total)

Timing Information:

Preparation	Cooking	Total Time
20 m	1 h 45 m	2 h 5 m

Nutritional Information:

Calories	329 kcal
Fat	3.6 g
Carbohydrates	56.5g
Protein	18.3 g
Cholesterol	0 mg
Sodium	317 mg

* Percent Daily Values are based on a 2,000 calorie diet.

EASY SAUSAGE AND LENTILS

Ingredients

- 1 (16 oz.) package dry lentils
- 1 (16 oz.) can diced tomatoes, drained
- 2 (14 oz.) cans beef broth
- 3 C. water
- 1 carrot, chopped
- 2 lbs kielbasa (Polish) sausage, cut into 1/2 inch pieces
- 1 stalk celery, chopped

Directions

- Run some fresh water over your lentils then place them in a crock pot with: celery, tomatoes, sausage, broth, carrots, and water.
- Place a lid on the slow cooker and let the contents cook for 3 hours on high or 8 hours on low. Stir then serve.
- Enjoy.

Amount per serving (12 total)

Timing Information:

Preparation	Cooking	Total Time
15 m	3 h	3 h 15 m

Nutritional Information:

Calories	357 kcal
Fat	21.2 g
Carbohydrates	22.8g
Protein	18.8 g
Cholesterol	50 mg
Sodium	966 mg

* Percent Daily Values are based on a 2,000 calorie diet.

Artisan Style Shiitake Mushrooms and Lentils

Ingredients

- 2 quarts vegetable broth
- 2 C. sliced fresh button mushrooms
- 1 oz. dried shiitake mushrooms, torn into pieces
- 3/4 C. uncooked pearl barley
- 3/4 C. dry lentils
- 1/4 C. dried onion flakes
- 2 tsps minced garlic
- 2 tsps dried summer savory
- 3 bay leaves
- 1 tsp dried basil
- 2 tsps ground black pepper
- salt to taste

Directions

- Add the following to a crock pot: salt, broth, pepper, mushrooms, basil, barley, bay leaves, lentils, savory, onion flakes, and garlic. Place a lid on the slow cook and cook for 6 hrs on high or 12 hrs on low.
- Enjoy.

Amount per serving (8 total)

Timing Information:

Preparation	Cooking	Total Time
15 m	12 h	12 h 15 m

Nutritional Information:

Calories	213 kcal
Fat	1.2 g
Carbohydrates	43.9g
Protein	8.4 g
Cholesterol	0 mg
Sodium	466 mg

* Percent Daily Values are based on a 2,000 calorie diet.

RUSTIC LENTILS WITH SAVORY CHICKEN

Ingredients

- 1 tbsp olive oil
- 2 lbs bone-in chicken pieces
- 1 large onion, finely chopped
- 1 small carrot, finely chopped
- 2 cloves garlic, finely chopped
- 3/4 C. dried lentils
- 1 (14 oz.) can chicken broth
- 1/2 tsp salt
- 1 (10 oz.) can tomato sauce
- 1/2 tsp dried rosemary
- 1/2 tsp dried basil
- 1 tbsp lemon juice

Directions

- Stir fry your chicken, in oil, in a big pot for 6 mins per side and then place the chicken to the side.
- Now stir fry your onions for 6 mins in the same pan and then add in the garlic, lentils, salt, broth, and carrots.
- Get everything boiling and then place a lid on the pot and cook for 22 mins over low heat.
- Now add back in, your chicken, and let the contents keep simmering for 20 more mins with a lid on the pot.
- Add water if needed then add in your tomato sauce, basil, and rosemary.
- Let the tomato sauce cook for 10 mins and finally combine in the lemon juice.
- Enjoy.

Amount per serving (6 total)

Timing Information:

Preparation	Cooking	Total Time
15 m	1 h 15 m	1 h 30 m

Nutritional Information:

Calories	308 kcal
Fat	13.5 g
Carbohydrates	18.7g
Protein	27.8 g
Cholesterol	68 mg
Sodium	816 mg

* Percent Daily Values are based on a 2,000 calorie diet.

Lentil Soup V

(Jalapenos, Black Beans, and Peppers)

Ingredients

- 1 lb dry black beans
- 1 1/2 quarts water
- 1 carrot, chopped
- 1 stalk celery, chopped
- 1 large red onion, chopped
- 6 cloves garlic, crushed
- 2 green bell peppers, chopped
- 2 jalapeno pepper, seeded and minced
- 1/4 C. dry lentils
- 1 (28 oz.) can peeled and diced tomatoes
- 2 tbsps chili powder
- 2 tsps ground cumin
- 1/2 tsp dried oregano
- 1/2 tsp ground black pepper
- 3 tbsps red wine vinegar
- 1 tbsp salt
- 1/2 C. uncooked white rice

Directions

- Submerge your beans in about 3 times their size of water.
- Then get everything boiling for 12 mins.
- Now place a lid on the pan and shut the heat.
- Let the beans sit for 1 and a half hours before removing the liquid and then rinsing the beans.

- Add your beans to a slow cooker with 1.5 quarts of fresh water and cook for 3 hrs on high.
- Now add the following after 3 hrs of cooking: tomatoes, carrots, lentils, celery, salt, chili powder, vinegar, cumin, black pepper, and oregano, jalapenos, onions, bell peppers, and garlic.
- With low heat cook for 3 more hrs. Then add the rice when about 25 mins is left in the cooking time.
- Take half of the soup and puree it in a blender then put it back in the pot.
- Enjoy.

Amount per serving (10 total)

Timing Information:

Preparation	Cooking	Total Time
1 h	5 h	6 h

Nutritional Information:

Calories	231 kcal
Fat	1.2 g
Carbohydrates	43.4g
Protein	12.6 g
Cholesterol	0 mg
Sodium	851 mg

* Percent Daily Values are based on a 2,000 calorie diet.

ARTISAN LENTIL BAKE

Ingredients

- 1 1/8 C. green lentils
- 2 1/4 C. water
- 6 slices white bread, torn into small pieces
- 2 eggs
- 1 C. vegetable broth
- 2 tbsps tomato paste
- 1/2 tsp dried basil
- 1/4 tsp garlic powder
- 1/2 tsp ground black pepper
- 1 tsp dried parsley
- 1 tbsp olive oil
- 1/2 packet dry vegetable soup mix
- 1/3 C. dried bread crumbs

Directions

- Boil your lentils and water for 3 mins then set the heat to low and let everything gently boil for 40 mins.
- Oil a bread pan and then set your oven to 400 degrees before doing anything else.
- Get a bowl, combine: soup mix, 2 C. of cooked lentils, olive oil, bread, parsley, eggs, black pepper, broth, garlic powder, tomato paste, and basil. Then enter everything into a bread pan.
- Cook the loaf in the oven for 40 mins. Then top with bread crumps and cook for 12 more mins. Let the contents cool for 15 mins before cutting.
- Enjoy.

Amount per serving (6 total)

Timing Information:

Preparation	Cooking	Total Time
45 m	50 m	1 h 35 m

Nutritional Information:

Calories	272 kcal
Fat	5.6 g
Carbohydrates	40.9g
Protein	14.6 g
Cholesterol	62 mg
Sodium	369 mg

* Percent Daily Values are based on a 2,000 calorie diet.

GREEK INSPIRED SALAD OF LENTILS

Ingredients

- 1 C. dry brown lentils
- 1 C. diced carrots
- 1 C. red onion, diced
- 2 cloves garlic, minced
- 1 bay leaf
- 1/2 tsp dried thyme
- 2 tbsps lemon juice
- 1/2 C. diced celery
- 1/4 C. chopped parsley
- 1 tsp salt
- 1/4 tsp ground black pepper
- 1/4 C. olive oil

Directions

- Get a big pot add in: thyme, lentils, bay leaves, carrots, garlic, and onions.
- Submerge everything in water then get it all boiling, set the heat to low, and cook for 22 mins with a light boil.
- Now remove all the liquid and the bay leaf.
- Pour in your olive oil, pepper, lemon juice, salt, celery, and parsley.
- Stir to evenly coat and serve when it has completely cooled off.
- Enjoy.

Amount per serving (8 total)

Timing Information:

Preparation	Cooking	Total Time
10 m	20 m	30 m

Nutritional Information:

Calories	147 kcal
Fat	7.1 g
Carbohydrates	16.2g
Protein	6 g
Cholesterol	0 mg
Sodium	453 mg

* Percent Daily Values are based on a 2,000 calorie diet.

South American Style Lentils (Peas, Apples, and Tomatoes)

Ingredients

- 1 C. dry lentils
- 1 quart water
- 1 cube vegetable bouillon
- 3 medium tomatoes, peeled and diced
- 1 large onion, diced
- 1 carrot, sliced
- 1 medium apple - peeled, cored and diced
- 1/2 C. frozen peas
- 1 large clove garlic
- 1 tbsp olive oil
- 1/4 C. barbeque sauce
- 1/2 tsp paprika
- salt and pepper to taste

Directions

- Boil the following, then simmer it over low heat, for 22 mins: water, veggie bouillon, and lentils.
- After 22 mins add in: paprika, tomatoes, bbq sauce, onions, olive oil, carrots, garlic, apple, and peas. Cook for 22 more mins.
- Then add your preferred amount of pepper and salt.
- Enjoy.

Amount per serving (4 total)

Timing Information:

Preparation	Cooking	Total Time
15 m	40 m	55 m

Nutritional Information:

Calories	266 kcal
Fat	4.3 g
Carbohydrates	46.3g
Protein	13.4 g
Cholesterol	0 mg
Sodium	225 mg

* Percent Daily Values are based on a 2,000 calorie diet.

Easy Ditalini Pasta

Ingredients

- 1 onion, chopped
- 3 cloves garlic, minced
- 2 tbsps olive oil
- 1 (19 oz.) can lentil soup
- 1 C. crushed tomatoes
- 1 (10 oz.) package frozen chopped spinach
- 1 (16 oz.) package ditalini pasta
- salt to taste
- ground black pepper to taste
- 1 pinch crushed red pepper
- 2 tbsps grated Parmesan cheese

Directions

- Fry your garlic and onions until browned and then add in your tomatoes and lentils. Get the mix boiling and add the spices and spinach.
- Simultaneously boil your pasta in water and salt for 9 mins. Then remove all the liquid. Now add it to the lentils. Place a lid on everything and cook it all over a very high heat for 22 mins.
- Enjoy.

Amount per serving (6 total)

Timing Information:

Preparation	Cooking	Total Time
15 m	30 m	45 m

Nutritional Information:

Calories	407 kcal
Fat	7.1 g
Carbohydrates	70.5g
Protein	15.9 g
Cholesterol	1 mg
Sodium	282 mg

* Percent Daily Values are based on a 2,000 calorie diet.

Portuguese Inspired Lentils

Ingredients

- 1 tbsp olive oil
- 2 cloves garlic, sliced
- 3/4 lb bulk chorizo sausage
- 5 ribs celery, sliced
- 1 C. dried lentils
- 3 C. water
- 1 tsp ground dried turmeric
- 1 tsp curry powder
- 1 tsp ground cumin
- salt and pepper to taste

Directions

- Stir fry your garlic for 1 min in olive oil in a big pot then add in your sausage and fry for 5 mins.
- Now add the celery and cook for 5 more mins continuing to stir and fry. Now combine in the water, cumin, curry, turmeric and lentils.
- Get everything boiling then place a lid on the pot and set the heat to low and let the contents gently boil for 40 mins.
- Add your preferred amount of pepper and salt and then serve. Enjoy.

Amount per serving (4 total)

Timing Information:

Preparation	Cooking	Total Time
10 m	50 m	1 h

Nutritional Information:

Calories	611 kcal
Fat	36.9 g
Carbohydrates	34.9g
Protein	33.9 g
Cholesterol	75 mg
Sodium	1145 mg

* Percent Daily Values are based on a 2,000 calorie diet.

COCONUT QUINOA

Ingredients

- 2 C. quinoa
- 3 1/2 C. water
- 1 tbsp salt
- 2 tbsps coconut oil
- 1 small onion, chopped
- 6 cloves garlic, minced
- 5 large tomatoes, chopped
- 1 C. water
- 1 (14 oz.) can coconut milk
- 1 tbsp molasses
- 1/4 C. coconut powder
- 1 (4 inch) cinnamon stick
- 3 tbsps curry powder
- 2 tbsps ground coriander
- 2 C. red lentils
- salt and pepper to taste
- 1 bunch fresh cilantro, chopped

Directions

- Submerge your quinoa in water, in a bowl, for 10 mins. Then remove all the liquid and run the quinoa under fresh cold water.
- Now boil the quinoa in 3.5 C. of water and 1 tsp of salt for 17 mins.
- Place a lid on the pan and cook with a lower level of heat.
- Stir fry your garlic and onions in coconut oil for 7 mins. Then add in the coconut milk and the water, coriander, molasses, curry powder, coconut powder, and cinnamon.
- Get everything boiling and then add the lentils and cook for 15 mins with a low level of heat.

- Make sure to stir every 3 to 5 mins.
- Now add your preferred amount of pepper and salt. Top with cilantro.
- Layer the lentils over the quinoa.
- Enjoy.

Amount per serving (12 total)

Timing Information:

Preparation	Cooking	Total Time
25 m	35 m	1 h

Nutritional Information:

Calories	347 kcal
Fat	13.5 g
Carbohydrates	45.5g
Protein	14.4 g
Cholesterol	0 mg
Sodium	602 mg

* Percent Daily Values are based on a 2,000 calorie diet.

LENTILS FROM GERMANY

Ingredients

- 2 C. dried brown lentils, rinsed and drained
- 3 C. chicken stock
- 1 bay leaf
- 1 C. chopped carrots
- 1 C. chopped celery
- 1 C. chopped onion
- 1 C. cooked, cubed ham
- 1 tsp Worcestershire sauce
- 1/2 tsp garlic powder
- 1/4 tsp freshly grated nutmeg
- 5 drops hot pepper sauce
- 1/4 tsp caraway seed
- 1/2 tsp celery salt
- 1 tbsp chopped fresh parsley
- 1/2 tsp ground black pepper

Directions

- Add the following to a crock pot: ham, lentils, pepper, Worcestershire, parsley, garlic powder, celery salt, nutmeg, caraway, hot sauce, onions, stock, carrots, and bay leaf.
- Place a lid on the slow cooker and let go for 9 hrs on low.
- Enjoy over cooked rice.

Amount per serving (8 total)

Timing Information:

Preparation	Cooking	Total Time
10 m	8 h	8 h 10 m

Nutritional Information:

Calories	221 kcal
Fat	2.3 g
Carbohydrates	34.2g
Protein	16 g
Cholesterol	10 mg
Sodium	608 mg

* Percent Daily Values are based on a 2,000 calorie diet.

Maggie's Easy Dahl

Ingredients

- 1 C. red lentils
- 2 tbsps ginger root, minced
- 1 tsp mustard seed
- 2 tbsps chopped fresh cilantro
- 4 tomatoes, chopped
- 3 onions, chopped
- 3 jalapeno peppers, seeded and minced
- 1 tbsp ground cumin
- 1 tbsp ground coriander seed
- 6 cloves garlic, minced
- 2 tbsps olive oil
- 1 C. water
- salt to taste

Directions

- Pressure cook the lentils until tender or boil them in water for 22 mins.
- Stir fry your mustard seeds until they being to pop then add in your oil, garlic, onions, jalapenos, and ginger.
- Continue stirring and frying until the onions are browned.
- Now pour in your tomatoes, cumin, and coriander.
- Cook the tomatoes for 2 mins and then add in your water and boil everything for 7 mins.

- Combine in your cooked lentils and mix everything.
- Finally add your preferred amount of salt.
- Serve with cilantro.
- Enjoy with cooked basmati.

Amount per serving (6 total)

Timing Information:

Preparation	Cooking	Total Time
10 m	40 m	50 m

Nutritional Information:

Calories	209 kcal
Fat	5.7 g
Carbohydrates	30.6g
Protein	10.4 g
Cholesterol	0 mg
Sodium	12 mg

* Percent Daily Values are based on a 2,000 calorie diet.

Savory Potatoes and Lentils

Ingredients

- 2 C. vegetable broth, divided
- 1 tsp yeast extract spread, e.g. Marmite/Vegemite
- 1/2 C. dry lentils
- 1/4 C. pearl barley
- 1 large carrot, diced
- 1/2 onion, finely chopped
- 1/2 C. walnuts, coarsely chopped
- 3 potatoes, chopped
- 1 tsp all-purpose flour
- 1/2 tsp water
- salt and pepper to taste

Directions

- Set your oven to 350 degrees before doing anything else.
- For 32 mins lightly boil: barley, 1.25 C. of broth, lentils, and yeast.
- Simultaneously simmer for 17 mins: walnuts, the rest of the broth, onions, and carrots. After the 17 mins is done add in your flour and water.
- Also at the same time boil your potatoes in water and salt for 17 mins. Then remove the liquid and mash them.

- Mix the carrots with the lentils.
- Add some pepper and salt and combine everything in a baking dish and top with the potatoes.
- Cook the contents in the oven for 32 mins.
- Enjoy.

Amount per serving (8 total)

Timing Information:

Preparation	Cooking	Total Time
15 m	1 h	1 h 15 m

Nutritional Information:

Calories	184 kcal
Fat	5.2 g
Carbohydrates	29.8g
Protein	6.2 g
Cholesterol	0 mg
Sodium	147 mg

* Percent Daily Values are based on a 2,000 calorie diet.

LENTILS AND CHARD WITH MUSHROOMS

Ingredients

- 1 tbsp olive oil
- 1 onion, diced
- 3 cloves garlic, minced
- 2 C. uncooked quinoa, rinsed
- 1 C. canned lentils, rinsed
- 8 oz. fresh mushrooms, chopped
- 1 quart vegetable broth
- 1 bunch Swiss chard, stems removed

Directions

- Stir fry your onions and garlic in a saucepan in oil for 7 mins. Add in the mushrooms, lentils, broth and quinoa.
- Get everything boiling and then place a lid on the pot and cook the contents with a lower level of heat for 20 mins.
- Shut the heat and add in your chards then stir to distribute them evenly.
- Place the lid back on the pot and let them sit for 7 mins.
- Enjoy.

Amount per serving (8 total)

Timing Information:

Preparation	Cooking	Total Time
20 m	20 m	40 m

Nutritional Information:

Calories	224 kcal
Fat	4.7 g
Carbohydrates	36.6g
Protein	9.6 g
Cholesterol	0 mg
Sodium	323 mg

* Percent Daily Values are based on a 2,000 calorie diet.

ITALIAN STYLE LENTILS WITH ZUCCHINI

Ingredients

- 2 tsps olive oil
- 1 C. chopped onion
- 2 C. fresh sliced mushrooms
- 1 small zucchini, chopped
- 3 cloves garlic, minced
- 1 C. dry lentils
- 3 C. water
- 2 (8 oz.) cans tomato sauce
- 1 (6 oz.) can tomato paste
- 1 1/2 tsps white sugar
- 1/2 C. water

Directions

- Stir fry, for 7 mins: garlic, onions, zucchini, and mushrooms. Then add in lentils and water (3 C.).
- Get everything boiling then lower the heat to a gentle boil and place a lid on the pot.
- Let everything cook for 40 mins.
- Now add in your tomato sauce and paste, half a C. of water, and your sugar.
- Get it all boiling again, lower the heat to low, and place a lid on the pot.
- Cook for 23 more mins and everything should be nice and thick.
- Enjoy with pasta.

Amount per serving (8 total)

Timing Information:

Preparation	Cooking	Total Time
20 m	1 h 20 m	1 h 40 m

Nutritional Information:

Calories	145 kcal
Fat	1.8 g
Carbohydrates	25.5g
Protein	8.9 g
Cholesterol	0 mg
Sodium	466 mg

* Percent Daily Values are based on a 2,000 calorie diet.

INDIAN STYLE POTATOES AND LENTILS

Ingredients

- 3 tbsps vegetable oil
- 1 1/2 pounds potatoes, cut into 1/2 inch dice
- 2 1/2 C. cauliflower florets
- 1 large onion, sliced
- 2 cloves garlic, crushed
- 1 tbsp curry powder
- 1/2 tbsp ground ginger
- 4 oz. dry red lentils
- 1 (14.4 oz.) can whole tomatoes, diced
- 1 1/4 C. vegetable stock
- 2 tbsps malt vinegar
- 1 tbsp mango chutney
- salt and pepper to taste
- diced fresh parsley for garnish

Directions

- Stir fry the following in oil until brown: potatoes, garlic, cauliflower, and onion.
- Add the ginger and curry and cook for 5 more mins.
- Now add: chutney, lentils, vinegar, stock, and tomatoes.
- Top everything with some pepper and salt and cook the mix with a lid on the pot for 22 mins.
- When serving add some parsley.
- Enjoy.

Amount per serving (4 total)

Timing Information:

Preparation	Cooking	Total Time
30 m	30 m	1 h

Nutritional Information:

Calories	395 kcal
Fat	11.4 g
Carbohydrates	62.9g
Protein	14 g
Cholesterol	0 mg
Sodium	272 mg

* Percent Daily Values are based on a 2,000 calorie diet.

THANKS FOR READING! NOW LET'S TRY SOME **SUSHI** AND **DUMP DINNERS**....

http://bit.ly/2443TFg

To grab this **box set** simply follow the link mentioned above, or tap the book cover.

This will take you to a page where you can simply enter your email address and a PDF version of the **box set** will be emailed to you.

I hope you are ready for some serious cooking!

http://bit.ly/2443TFg

You will also receive updates about all my new books when they are free.

Also don't forget to like and subscribe on the social networks. I love meeting my readers. Links to all my profiles are below so please click and connect :)

Facebook

Twitter

Interested in Other Easy Cookbooks?

Everything is easy! Check out my Amazon Author page for more great cookbooks:

For a complete listing of all my books please see my author page.

18765476R00095

Printed in Poland
by Amazon Fulfillment
Poland Sp. z o.o., Wrocław